What is a Solar Eclipse?

Have you ever played a game  fun game where you try to step on som solar eclipse is like a cosmic game of shadow tag played by the Sun, the Moon, and the Earth!

The Cosmic Game of Hide-and-Seek

A solar eclipse occurs when the Moon briefly blocks the Sun from our view, casting its shadow on Earth.

It's like the Moon is saying, "Hey Sun, you can't catch me!" and hides the Sun from our view. When this happens, it gets dark in the middle of the day, which is pretty amazing!

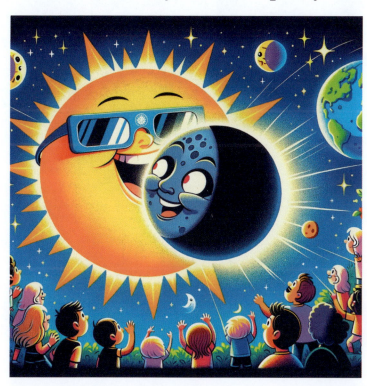

Total, Partial, and Annular Eclipses

There are different types of solar eclipses. In a total eclipse, the Moon completely obscures the Sun, causing a short period of darkness. Conversely, during a partial eclipse, only a portion of the Sun is covered by the Moon, resembling a crescent shape. And in an annular eclipse, the Moon is a bit too far from Earth to cover the whole Sun, so it looks like a ring of fire in the sky!

Solar Eclipse vs. Lunar Eclipse

Now, don't get solar eclipses mixed up with lunar eclipses. They're like cousins in the eclipse family! Earth's shadow sweeps across the Moon during a lunar eclipse, sometimes turning it a dramatic red, hence the nickname "Blood Moon." So, a solar eclipse is all about the Sun being hidden, while a lunar eclipse is about the Moon getting shadowy. Both are amazing natural shows, but in this book, we're going to focus on the exciting world of solar eclipses. Are you ready to learn more about how this incredible event happens? Let's go!

Types of Solar Eclipses

Imagine if every time you played hide-and-seek, the game was a little different. Sometimes you hid completely, sometimes only part of you was hidden, and sometimes you wore a special ring to make the game even more exciting. Well, that's kind of what happens with solar eclipses! There are different types, each with its own special twist.

Total Solar Eclipse: The Grand Show

A total solar eclipse is like the grand finale of a fireworks show. It's when the Moon completely covers the Sun, turning day into night for a few enchanting minutes. If you're in the path of a total eclipse, you might see stars and planets appear in the sky, and the temperature can even drop a bit. It's a rare and breathtaking sight!

Partial Solar Eclipse: A Sneaky Peek

A partial eclipse offers a glimpse, like peeking through a celestial curtain, as the Moon partially covers the Sun's dazzling display. It's like peeking through a curtain to see a bit of the show outside. The Sun looks like it has a chunk missing, but it's still important to wear special eclipse glasses to look at it safely.

Annular Solar Eclipse: The Ring of Fire
An annular solar eclipse is when the Moon is a little too far away from Earth to cover the whole Sun. Instead, it looks like a dark disk with a bright, fiery ring around it. That's why it's called an "annular" eclipse, which comes from the Latin word for ring. It's like the Sun is wearing a glowing crown!

Hybrid Solar Eclipse: A Bit of Everything

A hybrid solar eclipse is a special mix of a total and an annular eclipse. It's like a combo meal! Depending on where you are, you might see a total eclipse, an annular eclipse, or something in between. It's a rare event that keeps everyone guessing. So, whether it's a total, partial, annular, or hybrid eclipse, each type of solar eclipse brings its own unique magic to the sky. And the best part? You never know exactly what you're going to get until it happens!

How Does a Solar Eclipse Happen?

Have you ever wondered how all the planets and stars in the sky move around? It's like a giant dance in space! And sometimes, during this dance, the Sun, the Moon, and the Earth line up in a special way to create a solar eclipse. Let's find out how this happens!

The Perfect Alignment

Picture this: the Sun, the Moon, and the Earth are all playing a game of follow the leader. The Sun is the biggest and brightest, so it stays in one spot, shining its light. The Earth goes around the Sun in a big circle, like it's taking a long walk. And the Moon goes around the Earth, like it's playing tag. In a rare celestial alignment, the Moon positions itself directly between the Sun and Earth, casting its shadow upon our planet and creating the awe-inspiring spectacle known as a solar eclipse. It's like the Moon is saying, "Surprise!" and jumping out to block the Sun's light.

The Dance of Shadows

Now, let's use our imagination to picture how this works.

1. The Sun: Picture a big, bright ball of light. That's our Sun, staying in one spot and shining on everything.

2. The Earth: Now, imagine a smaller ball moving around the Sun in a big circle. That's the Earth, taking its yearly journey around the Sun.

3. The Moon: Finally, think of an even smaller ball moving around the Earth. That's the Moon, tagging along with the Earth on its journey.

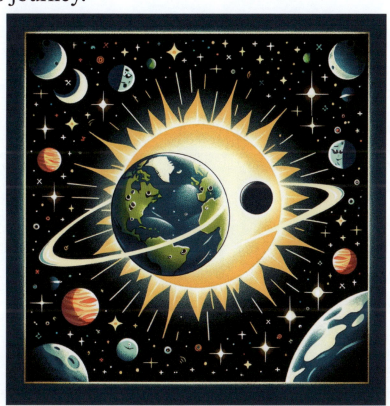

When the Moon moves right in front of the Sun and blocks its light, it's like the Moon is taking a turn to be the leader in the game. The shadow it casts on the Earth is what we see as a solar eclipse.

So, a solar eclipse is like a special moment in the dance of the Sun, the Moon, and the Earth when everything lines up just right. It's a reminder of how amazing and beautiful our universe is!

Viewing a Solar Eclipse Safely

Watching a solar eclipse is like being a part of a cosmic event! But just like we wear helmets when riding bikes or sunscreen at the beach, we need to protect ourselves when watching an eclipse. It's super important to remember one big rule: Never look directly at the Sun without proper protection!

Why Can't We Look at the Sun?
The Sun is incredibly bright, and looking at it without protection can hurt our eyes. During a solar eclipse, it might seem safe to look at the Sun when it's partly covered, but it's not. Even a tiny bit of the Sun's light can cause damage. So, we need to be careful and use the right gear to watch the eclipse safely.

Eclipse Glasses: Your Solar Shield

The best way to watch a solar eclipse is with special eclipse glasses. These aren't like regular sunglasses. They're much, much darker and are made to protect your eyes from the Sun's rays. When you wear them, you can look at the eclipse without worrying about hurting your eyes.

How to Use Eclipse Glasses:

1. Check the Glasses: Make sure there are no scratches or holes in the glasses.

2. Put Them On: Before you look up at the Sun, put the glasses on. Make sure they fit snugly and cover your eyes completely.

3. Look Up: Now you can safely look at the eclipse! Enjoy the view, but don't stare for too long.

4. Look Away: When you're done looking, turn your head away from the Sun before taking off the glasses.

The Science Behind Eclipses

Eclipses are not just beautiful and exciting to watch; they're also like a window into the secrets of the universe! Scientists use eclipses to learn more about the Sun, the Moon, and even the stars. Let's dive into some of the science behind eclipses.

Orbits: The Paths in Space

Everything in space moves in special paths called orbits. The Earth orbits, or goes around, the Sun, and it takes one year to complete this journey. The Moon takes roughly a month to circle Earth in its graceful orbit. These orbits are like invisible tracks in space, and they're the reason we have eclipses. When the Moon's orbit lines up just right with the Earth's orbit around the Sun, we get a solar eclipse!

Shadows: The Dark Side of Light

Light travels in straight lines, and when something blocks the light, it creates a shadow. A solar eclipse happens when the Moon perfectly positions itself between the Sun and Earth, casting its fleeting shadow on a particular area of our planet. This shadow is what creates the darkened phase of the eclipse that we observe.

The Moon's shadow isn't uniform. Its darkest region, called the umbra, is where the Sun is completely blocked, while the surrounding penumbra experiences partial shade. If you're in the path of the umbra, you'll see a total solar eclipse. The penumbra is a lighter shadow, where the Sun is only partially blocked. If you're in the penumbra, you'll see a partial solar eclipse.

Light: The Key to Understanding the Sun

When the Sun is fully obscured during a total solar eclipse, scientists have the opportunity to examine the Sun's outer atmosphere, known as the corona.

The corona is usually too dim to see because the Sun's bright surface outshines it. But during an eclipse, the corona becomes visible, and scientists can learn about its temperature, structure, and how it affects space weather.

Eclipses and Celestial Discoveries

Eclipses have helped scientists make some amazing discoveries. For example, during a total solar eclipse in 1919, scientists observed how the gravity of the Sun bent the light of distant stars. This observation supported Einstein's theory of relativity, which transformed the way we understand gravity and the mysterious universe! So, eclipses are not just fun to watch; they're also a way for scientists to explore the mysteries of space. Who knows what new discoveries might be made during the next eclipse?

Famous Solar Eclipses in History

Solar eclipses have been happening for as long as the Earth, Sun, and Moon have been around. People from different cultures and times have witnessed these amazing events, and they've often had some pretty interesting reactions. Let's take a look at some famous solar eclipses from history and see how people reacted to them.

The Eclipse That Stopped a War

One of the earliest recorded eclipses happened in 585 B.C. in what is now Turkey. According to the ancient Greek historian Herodotus, two warring kingdoms, the Lydians and the Medes, were in the middle of a battle when suddenly, day turned into night. The soldiers were so shocked by the sudden darkness that they stopped fighting and agreed to make peace. This eclipse is known as the "Eclipse of Thales," named after the philosopher who supposedly predicted it.

The Emperor Who Was Scared of the Dark

In ancient China, eclipses were seen as warnings from the heavens. The Chinese believed that a dog was eating the Sun, and they would bang drums and make loud noises to scare the dog away. One famous story is about Emperor Zhong Kang, who was so unprepared for an eclipse that he hadn't arranged for the usual rituals to be performed. The eclipse was seen as a bad omen, and the emperor was so embarrassed that he had the astronomers who failed to predict it executed!

The Eclipse That Changed Science

In more recent history, the total solar eclipse of 1919 is one of the most famous. This was the eclipse that helped prove Albert Einstein's theory of relativity. During the eclipse, astronomers measured the positions of stars near the Sun, and they found that the stars appeared to be in slightly different places than expected. This was because the gravity of the Sun bent the light from the stars, just like Einstein's theory predicted. This discovery was a big deal in the world of science and made Einstein a superstar.

Eclipses in Myth and Legend

Different cultures have their own stories and legends about eclipses. In many Native American tribes, an eclipse is seen as the Sun and Moon having a disagreement. In Vietnamese culture, it's believed that a giant frog is swallowing the Sun.

And in Norse mythology, the wolves Skoll and Hati chase the Sun and Moon, and when they catch them, an eclipse happens. For millennia, solar eclipses have captivated humanity, sparking wonder, fear, and countless stories. They've stopped wars, changed science, and inspired countless myths and legends. Who knows what stories will be told about the next big eclipse?

Fun Facts About Solar Eclipses

1. Speedy Shadows: During a total solar eclipse, the Moon's shadow moves across the Earth's surface at speeds of up to 1,700 miles per hour!

2. A Rare Sight: Total solar eclipses happen about once every 18 months somewhere on Earth, but they're only visible from a small area. So, seeing one from your hometown is pretty rare!

3. Eclipse Chasers: Some people love solar eclipses so much that they travel around the world to see them. They're called "eclipse chasers," and they go wherever they need to be to catch a glimpse of this celestial event.

4. Animal Reactions: During a total solar eclipse, animals can get confused. Birds might stop singing, thinking it's night, and some animals might head to bed!

Myths and Legends

The mysterious phenomenon of solar eclipses has captivated humanity for thousands of years, with various cultures weaving tales of celestial dogs devouring the sun, angry gods plunging the world into darkness, and even prophesies of impending doom.

The Quarreling Sun and Moon: Some Native American tribes thought that a solar eclipse happened when the Sun and Moon were fighting. They saw it as a time to come together and resolve conflicts.

The Romantic Reunion: In some African myths, a solar eclipse is seen as the Sun and Moon coming together in a romantic reunion, reminding people of the importance of love and harmony.

Whether it's a scientific phenomenon or a magical event from a storybook, solar eclipses have a way of capturing our imagination and reminding us of the wonders of the universe. So the next time you witness an eclipse, remember the amazing facts and the enchanting stories that have been told about this celestial event throughout history!

The Wonder of Eclipses

Solar eclipses are more than just a rare and beautiful sight. They remind us of the incredible world we live in and the wonders of the cosmos. Throughout history, they have sparked curiosity, inspired stories, and advanced our understanding of the universe.

Witnessing a solar eclipse offers a unique opportunity to observe the intricate movements of our solar system, a testament to the delicate balance and powerful forces at play in the universe.

If you ever have the chance to see one, remember to do so safely, with proper eye protection. It's a celestial event you won't want to miss! So, keep your eyes to the skies and get ready for the next solar eclipse.

Visit our author page for more children's books, and remember to follow us for updates on new releases, including illustrated storybooks, fun-fact picture books, coloring books, activity books for kids, and more:

Amazon.com/author/88

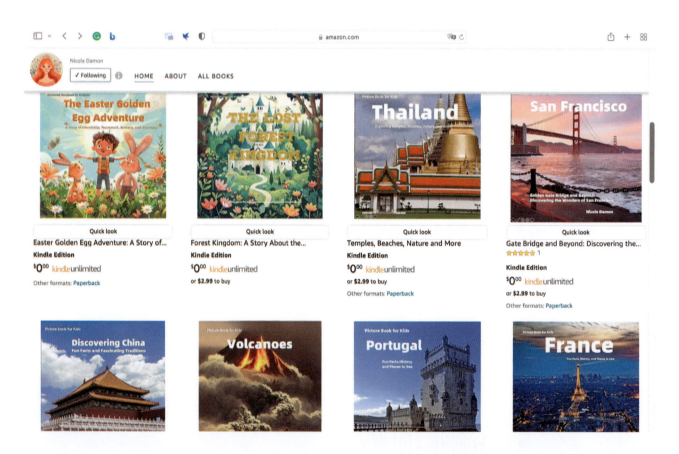

Printed in Great Britain
by Amazon